I0182549

COMMON

GREENS

By A.M. Sherwin

COMMON GREENS

©2011 A.M. Sherwin.   All rights reserved.

ISBN: 978-0-578-07766-6

No part of this book may be reproduced or transmitted in any form or by any means, electronic or mechanical, including photocopying, recording, or by any information storage and retrieval system, without written permission from the publisher.

PUBLISHED BY HAPPY MEDIA, LLC

www.happymedia.com

800.813.8953

For Margaret and Henry

Suggested Soundtrack

Kids, MGMT

Let the Drummer Kick, Citizen Cope

Airplanes, B.O.B

Human, The Killers

Embrace the Martian, Kid Cudi

Get Busy Living or Get Busy Dying, Fall Out Boy

Forest Whitaker, Brother Ali

Bleed American, Jimmy Eat World

Burn This City, Cartel

I Just Wanna Run, The Downtown Fiction

Wet Hot American Summer, Cobra Starship

Live Your Life, T.I.

Stronger, Kanye West

The Curse of Curves, Cute is what we aim for

Hollywood, Cute is what we aim for

The Take Over The Break's Over, Fallout Boy

Bang the Doldrums, Fallout Boy

False Pretense, Red Jumpsuit Apparatus

Simple Man, Lynyrd Skynyrd

Opposite of Adults, Chiddy Bang

The Beginning

It was a wet day in early May. They had kept us indoors until the bulk of the rain had gone, but there were washouts everywhere, and more than a few puddles. My partner in the Thursday Night League and I were in our golf cart, about 60 yards from the 6th Green, on the path at the top of the hill. He turned the cart to the right off the path towards his ball, which was through the edge of the woods on the green side.

Almost immediately, the brakes locked and we began to slide. Down the hill, the rear of the cart swinging forward as we turned backwards.

"Holy shit!"

"Brake, brake, brake!"

The cart spun once. It spun again and nearly tipped. It swung once more, and then settled into a steady and true line.

"Holy shit! I've got kids, you know!" I shouted.

Backwards. We were moving backwards about as fast as a golf cart can travel, downhill, toward the woods on the left side of the 7th Hole, and the Brook beyond, for which the Course is known.

"Bail!", my partner shouted.

"Bail!, Bail!", he shouted again, while preparing to leave the stricken golf cart.

I was thinking the same thing, (though he later claimed to have saved my life), and I took a quick look at the slick hill as we slid towards the hard trees. I took a breath, braced myself, and dove away from the cart the only direction I could, onto my twice surgically-repaired right shoulder.

*

I made a small fire in my backyard. I retrieved my branding iron, and turned my plastic Adirondack chair towards the south. Over the neighbors' barn, back towards the city.

Fall had arrived, though it didn't feel like it.

It was a little too warm and steamy, but that wasn't likely to last for long. This time of year, my thoughts often turn back towards the typing. It was time. Have you ever read Wodehouse or Updike's golf writing? Because my golf stuff is just like theirs. Just much less funny, less interesting, and not as well-written.

This isn't exactly a pageturner. Probably good for reading on the can. Or a bus. It's brief.

*

This is the story, among other things, of one round of golf, my attempt to become one of the few golfers (relative to the overall golfing population) to break 80 on a regulation Par 72 course. Golf is a funny game.

When I began this project, it was something else entirely called "Heavy Static". It was only about halfway through that it became clear that this was another story altogether. The last few pages of this section are a little preview of that tale not yet told.

As a result, this volume is, in my humble opinion, sorely lacking in hahas. To partially make up for this condition, I have included 4 pages of classic Standup Comedy bits from the 70s at the end. Just kidding, you're stuck with more of my yammering internal monologue. But we'll soon get to the golf.

However, if you skip around enough, you'll encounter 18 Holes of golf, a good deal of skiing, some witty repartee, vertigo, Pars, Bogies, a birdie, and even reference to the title of the book.

But really, here's a joke:

*

A horse walks into a bar.

The bartender asks "Why the long face?"

The horse does not respond, because it is a horse. It can neither speak nor understand English.

It is confused by its surroundings and gallops out of the bar, knocking over a few tables.

*

If nothing else, Common Greens is half as long, and twice as good, as my first book. So I've got that going for me. Which is nice. (There. Another joke. A golf one even. Not one of mine, but still.)

What this slim volume does have is my best effort, for the moment, to capture my love of this ancient game, and my views on how the game benefits those who devote some time and attention to it. Some of my best times have been golf-related. This game is something that has been passed down from generation to generation, and while it is ultimately trivial in the grand scheme of things, I'd like to see my kids take it up, to whatever end.

*

One of your Great-Great-Grandfathers was the Methodist Bishop of Burma. Another wrote books about some of the more important political and public events of the 20th Century. He also played the game of golf. There is a picture in my office of the golfer's wife, who was your Great-Grandmother, and her brother. They are about your age, and they look just like you two.

About the game: you've got to hit the ball straight, in order to play well. Or if not straight, then at least on its intended line. And an accumulation of shots that do, or do not, keep to their intended line, are what makes up a round of golf. So go ahead and hit that worm burner, that pop up. They will wind up in the center of the hole, and give you more opportunities to make up the ground you've just lost. That's the thing though: try to make up some ground after a wasted shot, and you will soon have even more to make up. You've got to have the discipline to accept each shot as its own, and to approach the next shot as if it were the first.

*

My car died, on the way to the bank. You won't remember it (you are 3 1/2 and 1 1/2 when this book is first published), but it was a 1991 Volvo 940 Turbo Wagon. I purchased it in August of 2007. It is now October of 2010. The car cost us $2,000, and I drove it for 3 years and more than 21,000 miles.

Once a month, I have to make the 75 mile round-trip to Pawling, NY, to deposit a check or cash to cover the mortgage. The most direct route from here in Litchfield involves an unpaved road for about a mile, up a large hill near where our county becomes Dutchess County. I do this because the bank that holds our checking account and mortgage has its nearest Branch all the way over there, and its seems best to keep thing all in the corporate family.

*

Henry, you sure seem to love the music. It's early, but you demand that we turn on the radio whenever we enter the house. You boogie, sure...but it seems more than that. In any event, like most typers, I'm a frustrated something. Music does it for me most days, and I do wish I had some skills along those lines. I'd make a fantastic Radio DJ, if such a thing really existed anymore, but it's far too late for me to learn to actually create music. At this point, as I have been saying so often lately, I am who I am.

I remember making some rudimentary tunes with my Casio MT-68. I was closer than I realized to making what would now be considered music. A canned beat, an endlessly repeated hook, and some complimentary riffs. Maybe 25 years of memory distorts (ha!), but I feel like I remember putting those elements together more than a few times before my total lack of actual piano playing ability discouraged me from pursuing the process further. Little did I know that crafting beats, and hooks, and riffs, would quite soon thereafter become all one needed to make big music. But fuck that...learn to play some instruments, like your Uncle Taya, and you'll be able to do a lot with that creative energy. Every time I find myself here at my desk in the wee hours of the morning, typing away with the music turned up wicked loud, I wonder what it would be like to be composing songs instead of paragraphs.

*

More so than living in the city, where everything is provided for you, living up here in the country provides daily stark reminders of the fact that we currently rely far too heavily on other people and organizations to bring us the things we need to live comfortably. There is a large-format book in our kitchen titled:

Country Wisdom & Know-How

8,167 USEFUL SKILLS AND STEP-BY-STEP INSTRUCTIONS INCLUDING:

Attracting Hummingbirds * Baking Basic Bread *
Breeding Livestock * Building Homebrew Equipment *
Caning Chairs * Concocting Elixers and Remedies *
Constructing a Chicken Coop...

You get the idea. Several of our neighbors have
their own chicken coops, which they (of course)
constructed themselves. Now that is some serious
business. In the event of a disruption in the systems that
bring us our stuff, these people would be prepared. To
have their cholesterol raised? I'm not sure that they are
much readier than we are for a less-secure tomorrow...but
that gives me no confidence.

1

Tonight is the Banquet for the Francis Fiolek Memorial Tuesday Night Golf League. This was my first year in the league, which has been going on since the 1960s. My playing partner in the league is Mikey, the Senior member of the Course Maintenance Staff. I am grateful to him for the opportunity to play in the league, since usually someone has to die. His previous partner, Dewey, is quite old, but I still see him driving around town. I frequently pass by Dewey's house and car on my way back from Mohawk Mountain, our local ski hill.

I was in three leagues this year (2010). In the Friday night league, I once witnessed the following exchange, word for word.

Player 1, holding a pose and staring down another smother-hooked drive, "I think I might be the worst player in this whole league."

His partner replied, without a pause, hesitation, or qualification, "You are".

*

This 1st Hole is a 380 Yard Par 4 that plays downhill, and fairly straight away. I use my Adams Golf XTD Pro 14.5" Hybrid, and hit a low, looping push down the right side. It was well hit, and dead straight, just about 10 yards too far right to stay in the fairway and setup a birdie opportunity. Now I am scrambling, but the ball should wind up somewhere not too bad.

The ball, a Bridgestone E7, is marked with the initials of my children. It comes to rest on an extension of the cart path made up of paver-sized granite rocks. Free drop within one club-length. The nearest point of relief is mostly under a tree just off the fairway, and I am left with a fairly bare lie. There is a bunker in between my location and the hole, which I do not want to mess with at this early stage, from this sort of hairy spot.

If you spend some time at a place where people work, get to know them and their work. It is important to have empathy for your fellow people, and one of the best ways to do this, and show it, is to understand the good and bad of their work life. Family is important, art is important, sport is important, but we spend an awful lot of our time working. And the clearest path to gaining most people's respect is to be familiar with the work they do when you are not working.

*

Prior to the Banquet, I'll be playing a match with three other members of the league, J, S, and M. I have played practice rounds with M, and a scramble tournament with S. The very first match I ever played, in the First Round of our Club Championship, was against J. He had been our Club Champ 7 times, and had played in some

State Amateur events. I lost that first match 8 & 6, which is just about what you'd expect.

I've only been playing the game for five years. I play frequently, but when you stick that tee into the ground, on the first hole, there is always a moment of pure panic. Especially when playing with or against good, experienced players. On this day, I had hit exactly 4 balls on the range beforehand. Uncharacteristically, I had striped each one of them. I am usually a bit of a slow starter. I had also spent a little extra time on and around the practice green.

The course we were playing that day sits up on and around a hill on the site of a former farm. The first four holes play down, then up, then down, then farther down the East side of the hill. The fifth hole plays North on the far Eastern boundary of the property. Six and seven play West back up the hill, then eight and nine play down and up once again to the clubhouse. The back nine is a bit more of a jumble, with more variety to the direction and slope of the holes.

As a result of this, a lot of people find it tough to keep a good round going after a strong front nine, or find their games picking up in the second half if they have been struggling.

2

I need to get the ball in the air. But I also need to avoid those overhead branches. If I get the ball on the ground towards the left side of the green, it will head back towards the right, towards the pin. If it stays short, it'll be in the run-up area, where I can hopefully chip it close.

Can't go long here down the hill into the woods, but I sure as hell don't want to stub the pitch and leave it back up here. Need clean contact. Nothing fat or thin. Punchy.

3

Chip from the run-up area, runs a little long. Not a great shot, but not a bad miss.

This is, ultimately, the way to be a better golfer, a better...most things. Incremental improvement, and the lessening of the impact of mistakes. In this case, a mediocre shot probably cost me the opportunity to make par. However, the shot was good enough that I am not likely to make worse than bogie.

Sure there are analogies to be made here about many other aspects of life and sport. However, I am not drunk enough at the moment to get into them without the mortification of one who feels, rightly or wrongly, that they've been going on and on, about very little. So fuck off if you were expecting much of that. Mostly, all you're gonna get is more of this semi-interior inner golf telecast.

Or are you? No, really. You are.

4

Good putt, doesn't quite hold its line. Speed plays a remarkable factor in avoiding three-putts. Most people can more-or-less read the general intended direction of a putt. But speed is mostly feel and practice. You can't line up speed. But if you can consistently get the speed right on the green, you'll leave yourself with much more make-able second putts.

And it is this part of the mental game of golf that is so frequently overlooked. Which is why children, and rank amateurs, can at times seem to excel at this part of the game. It's all feel with them. They are not trying to execute any sort of putting thought. They are just trying to get the ball in the hole.

5

I am left with a two-footer, maybe a little more. I go into my brief, if deliberate routine, even after S. concedes the putt. I'm like that. Especially early in the round.

S says, authoritatively, "If you don't take a putt that is offered, you lose the hole."

I scoop the ball up, and head back to the golf cart.

There is something about the rhythm of a golf game, the structure and the players creating a singular little dance step. Even in this age of perpetual OCD phone-checking and 6 hour rounds and techno-jargon, the game manages to simplify all the other backwash in one's head. It took X amount of strokes to get from this spot to that spot. This other person, it took him 1 fewer stroke. Another person took two more than I did. Another the same as I did. The structure of the game sharpens the reality of what each of us is doing in that moment, on that day, in that place, with those people, in between work, family, other sports, entertainment, drama, life.

*

I got my first set of golf clubs (from my wife Amey) for my 29th Birthday, a few months after our wedding.

Not wanting to embarrass myself too badly on the course, I spent the winter (or, more accurately, Mid-

September until Late January) sweating at the driving range. Once I felt comfortable enough, I prepared to play.

My chance came on January 26, at the Key West (FL) Golf Club. When we arrived in town, I made myself an early morning tee-time, so as to best protect my previously untested game from the judging eyes of the golfing public. I hit a few balls in the small cage-like range at the attractive club, and in the dewy early morning light, I teed it up.

6

With my 3-wood/hybrid, I hit a low liner on this 2nd Tee. This Hole is a 355-Yard Par 4 that plays entirely uphill, back towards the clubhouse and the Hole we just played.

My ball gets farther out there than it looked, and is right in the middle of the fairway. This why I usually hit my 3-wood off the tee. I would always rather my miss lose distance, but still be on the right line. When I hit driver, my misses wind up in worse places. This is usually because I hit it pretty hard, just not quite on the right line. Or, my weight stays back, and I hit the Big Right Block, which is essentially the same thing.

This is a situation where I should almost certainly be hitting a hybrid or wood off the fairway. 220 yards, uphill, into the wind. I just don't trust that shot yet, in a stroke play situation. I like my chances of punch-running a 3-iron up the hill better than taking some unfamiliar swing with my 14.5 degree hybrid. I am just a much better iron player overall. Since the second shoulder surgery, I do try to stick with one swing as much as possible.

7

3-iron hit hard, runs up the hill, but not as far as I thought. Uncharacteristically, I leave the cart with just my putter. I'm almost always careful to bring a wedge with me if there is any chance whatsoever that I may need to chip. I use my wedge in places that many other people would not.

8

I hustle back to the cart to get my 56 degree wedge, and wind up hitting a poor, poorly thought-out pitch/chip. Leaving myself in lag range.

I rushed the shot, and did not have a clear idea of what I was trying to do. This a classic high handicapper short game mistake. Though my chipping is often good, it's not unusual for me to leave a chip short. But it is unusual for me to leave a chip this far short, for no good reason.

9

I have a 20 foot putt, moving right to left. For Par. It's a little bit uphill, so I am going to have to Hit it, to get it to the hole. I had the right idea, but not the right execution. I stroke a fairly indifferent putt, as my mind was still focused on the poor chip I had just hit. All in all, however, not a terrible start to the round if I can sink this next putt.

10

3 footer right up the hill. Good stroke. Making 3-footers for bogie is no way to go through life. Some days, you need to make a few of these type of Putts to get things going. And at the level I play at (and most amateurs), bogie is our friend.

So go ahead, make that bogie. You can make a few Pars or a birdy, and get right back on track towards a good round. It is the double-bogies, triple bogies, and others that are very difficult to get away with if we want to shoot in the 70s or low 80s.

*

The first time I ever broke 100 was at Harbor Links Golf Course in Port Washington, Long Island, New York. It is a very nicely maintained public course, fairly wide open, but with a lot of waste areas, wildlife protection areas, and other hazards for the rank amateur. I played the course from the White Mens Tees, which are at a length of 6490 Yards, a Course Rating of 71.0, and a Slope of 125.

The last Hole at this particular course is a dogleg left Par-4 with a housing development all along the right side. Naturally, being a bit nervous, I pulled my first drive off of one of the aforementioned houses. My next drive was centered, and reasonably well hit. I somehow coaxed the ball up towards the green, on the left side, and avoided the trap on that side. My chip ran well long, and I two-putted for a triple-bogie. A quick tally of the numbers on the scorecard told me that I had shot an honest 99. No gimmes, no mulligans, no bullshit.

*

In Fall of the year prior to my first year playing golf, I used to spend half an hour or so every evening chipping balls, ever so delicately, onto the small leather couch in the living room of our apartment in Astoria.

Open the face, slide it under the ball. It pops up, more up than forward, and settles softly on the slippery, unflat surface of the couch. On a good day, little shots like these can really improve the old scorecard.

*

There is a Country Club just up the street from our house. It has 9 Holes, a Pool, and Tennis Courts, and frequently hosts events. I have only played there once, and while its golf course is not as challenging as my own home course across town, I look forward to maybe walking down there with my kids on some Summer evenings in the not-too-distant future. Though right at the moment, I'd settle for having my clients pay us what they owe. On time, or something closer to it.

11

There is Out of Bounds right on this 3rd Hole, so I am aiming left with my 3-wood/hybrid, and the ball stays there. This is a downhill slightly left-to-right 500 yard Par 5. It is reachable in two shots by many players.

Not a bad drive overall for this hole, but I need to play from the fairway to play well. Because of my short game, and because the low roller I usually hit delivers the sort of performance I need much better on short grass then it does in the rough. I am in play though, and on this hole as long we stay in play for two shots, and advance the ball, we should be able to hit the green in regulation.

12

Not a bad spot, but not a great lie. I punch it, a little too close to the tree on the left for comfort, but safely advanced. Little successful executions of the gameplan like this one can have huge, far reaching consequences over the course of a round, and a season.

13

It's got to be a Pitching Wedge or a 9-iron. The back of the green drops off into woods. There is also a trap on the right, and another drop-off, albeit a lesser one, off the left side of the green.

Oddly, I ask my cart partner, J, whether I should hit Wedge or 9-iron. I've only played golf with this fellow a few times, so he has no idea whether this is the right club. He is not familiar enough with my game to accurately make that assessment.

"Can I hit the 9 here? I don't want to go long on this one".

"Yep...I like that club.", he says.

I think to myself, "Self, better get some air under it. No screamers. You hit a low liner here and this ball will surely be lost."

I yank it a little, but it finishes about 20 feet left, hole high.

14

I am squarely in coax mode. This is one of the advantages of hitting fairways and greens. Makes two-putts perfectly good for Pars.

Left to right a few feet, needs some pace, but these greens are slick. All about speed. Get it right and the hole appears.

I don't make many birdies. But when I play well, I don't make many double-bogies or worse. I can make a lot of pars, and when playing well I can minimize the damage, and keep the mistake bogies. With my game, I am in no danger of shooting in the 60s, but with continued improvement I may well possess a legit single-digit handicap. This is the goal of millions of golfers.

*

The first birdie I ever made was at Egremont Golf Course in The Berkshires. The second hole is a short, driveable Par-4. It's right along the road, so if you miss your drive to the right, you just might get yourself a windshield on Route 23. I remember hitting a not-so-great drive (with the anti-right swing), but hitting a good approach to about 6 feet, and making the putt.

I have driven past this golf hole more than any other, I suspect, since it is just a few minutes from my in-laws house, and the place where I went to school.

*

I like it up here in the country, and I try to take a walk into town every single day. My daughter Maggie and I usually go for a walk around 3 in the afternoon most weekdays, sometimes up North Street to the Sarah Pierce sign, sometimes just to the wine shop, most days to the library, but always, always up South Street, into the center of town.

*

Well, Volume 1 went just about as well I could have hoped. On time, mostly on message, and I covered a lot of ground. Enough ground, hopefully, that the many references to that Volume, in all my subsequent work, will force anyone not already in possession of Greetings from Astoria (which is just about everyone but me and my mother-in-law) to immediately run out and acquire it. Daycare is expensive, and we could use the $20 bucks.

*

But back to the task at hand. Short of getting all orange robed and hanging out at airports, what are the ways in which we can part the curtain? How do we eliminate, or greatly reduce, the Heavy Static?

No. Like most of us, I like to fast forward. To a time when the absence of the noise, the lack of static, is very loud. Every morning, I wake at 5:30. I'm in boots and jeans and a jacket by 5:45, and out the door. I'm down the hill, and into the woods toward Little Pond. By the time I'm there, I've got a good head of steam, my pulse and breathing are elevated, and the static, what little remains in this country life, fades out.

Walking meditation of this sort is, ultimately, my only option. You can take the boy out of Jersey, but you can't take Jersey out of the boy. Here I sit, writing while drinking (cola) while watching the game while watching the people. And now, the next afternoon under my sweater I'm wearing a t-shirt my wife got me for Xmas, which reads "Everything I know I learned in Jersey". Not true...but I like the idea.

An example, of sorts: if I'm crashing with a friend, or for some other reason couch-bound for the evening...I sleep just fine. But at home, on a king-size pillow-top, it takes hours to put me down. Is this a sleep number issue?

Or is this a multimedia issue, related to the need to have the tv on in the background when I'm working? None of it will impact the price of gas, and none of it matters on the golf course.

Back to Volume 1: You see, there was so much stuff that I absolutely had to shoehorn into any first HM-related book. Since you never know if your first...will be your last. This one, on the other hand, is different. I've said all the things I *have* to say...to get them off my chest. About modern life, about the technology that rules it, and about how to get back to that which was good and right and natural old school, agrarian living. The lack of heavy static. The clarity of vision. The quiet upper body. Wait, no...that's skiing.

*

I remain a grinder. I grind away, day after day, inefficiently and without pause. Hoping to make up in volume what I lose by working away like this, day after day, without too much of a plan or anywhere near an appropriate budget. And yes, after nearly 10 years it should occur to me that that is, in actuality, the ideal budget to with which to create: just enough to generate the required background noise for proper, for improper, creation. It would, almost without question, be better if I painted instead.

Like Buk said, and Donleavy... it's easy to write like that when you've just had a nice steak dinner, with some good whiskey and a nice cola for digestion. And it's true... this is the ideal environment for creative work, no matter the medium. It's harder when you've just made a payment to keep the electric on, and the landlord has just taped an eviction notice to the front door.

*

In the my new vehicle, a Silver 2001 VW Jetta with black leather interior, there is a problem with the right rear speaker. The only noise coming out of the speaker is a steady, slightly urgent hiss, like the kind you used to get from a broadcast TV Station that wasn't coming in correctly.

The thing is...the hiss seems to be there whenever the car is running, whether the radio/cd is on or not. It's the last thing that you hear when you turn the car off, and it leaves a lingering hollow ache in my right ear. Some moments, it gets so that I miss the hiss, and I listen for it when listening to music at my desk, or when I'm in another vehicle, or when I'm at the bar.

That's what the background noise of a good run of golf is like...Heavy Static. No swing though good or bad, no thoughts of the car payment, the leaky roof, the illnesses and injuries to ones body, mind, and heart.

*

My wife and I took a 12-day odyssey throughout New England about 5 years ago. During the trip I turned 30, Summer Ended, and I played 7 rounds of golf in 12 days at 5 different courses in 4 State/Provinces in 2 countries. We went from NYC to Great Barrington, MA, to Hillsboro, NH, to Rockport, ME, to Quebec City, QE to South Royalton, VT, to Windsor, CT to New Haven, CT, then finally home.

*

The 18-Hole Country Club in the next town over recently had their Clubhouse burn down. As a result of that calamity, and declining numbers overall, they are having a One-Year Special Membership available to members of other clubs.

I would only do it if I could do both. Great course, great facility (even after the fire), but you gotta be true to your school. And Stonybrook is the place where I learned the most about how to play the game. It's got a lot more character, and a lot more characters, than most places. Like something out of Dan Jenkins, or Bukowski, though not much out of Wodehouse or Donleavy.

And ultimately, that's the combination I am trying, and a the moment, failing, to capture. The humor and ego-less amusement of Jenkins, with the history, legacy, and timelessness of Wodehouse. With some of the nihilistic aspects of the Buk. Good luck, asshole. You ain't no Updike, Jenkins, or Wodehouse. And you're way to goddamn conventional to channel Henry Chinaski. After all, the only people gonna read this are your wife, a few of your friends, one or two of your more literate drinking buddies, and eventually, when you kick off early, your kids.

There's something undeniably attractive about having a modest 9-hole course be your golf home. When a movie is "based on the true story", they would inevitably have the protagonist hail from, if not a pitch-and-putt, then at the very least a no-frills, jeans wearing, bud heavy drinking, ball-busting, CL&P League hosting, no cart-girl-having, pick your own playing partners, the-tee-is-open 9-holer.

15

Today the 4th Hole is just about 185 Yards, playing downhill. J's tee shot on this suddenly a bit longer Par 3 runs long and over the back. Mine, a five-iron, stays true to roughly the same line, but stays on the green. Now that I have played this game for 5 years, I do sometimes receive a benefit from seeing what a player does before my shot. Especially if I have played with a player before, I'm able to gauge what the shot needs to be. A good player can see what needs to be done, and execute the shot. I can do this some of the time. This makes me an almost good player. This is reflected in my handicap.

16

Not leaving these short any more. Misses though. There is no question that as a good player, you need to get more Putts to the hole. If they miss, you get to see what they do around the hole. With the exception of Putts that are exceptionally downhill, or leading onto a lower tier, this holds true of most putts for birdie or par. And hell, if you're making worse than bogie, might as well give it a run.

17

Go in the hole. It does. J with a world-class up-and-down. This is the second hole in a row that we have hit the green in regulation, and then made Par or better. A good player can get on a run of these, and it leads to lower scores. Makes up for some bogies, and gives one just the right air of blithe confidence that one needs to play well for a string of holes.

*

During one freak round during my first year playing golf, I shot 84 on a Par 67 Course. Douglaston Golf Course in Queens, NY may not be the longest or toughest course. But it has some serious twists, turns, and surprisingly, some substantial changes in elevation. So you have to do some things right in order to shoot a number like that. You have to make Pars in bunches, and avoid the doubles, triples, and others that really savage a scorecard.

*

I have been trying to write like Fante lately. But I think like Baker, so it is hard. Also, contrary to what my family, friends, etc may lead you to believe, I don't have that much to say. So stringing together hundreds of these little bits and pieces is more difficult than typing about nothing should be.

*

No question about it. I take it all back. It is easier to put one honest word in front of another, to whatever end, when there is nothing else that you can afford to do. At the moment, I have $12 in cash, and a total of about $50 on 3 debit cards. And no credit cards. So, since I need the remaining funds for gas, my daughters trips to the coffee shop over the nest few days, and have no idea when

(before next Thursday, 11 days away) more dough will

arrive, it is very easy to sit here and keep typing.

18

I once again go to my 3-wood/hybrid on this 5th Hole, a somewhat short, left-to-right dogleg Par-4. There is a pond on the player's right, and fairway bunkers just off the fairway in the preferred landing area. The tee shot wanders a little too far right, but we're not quite blocked out. I have got a Gap wedge in my hand, which is nice. But I will need to be precise. The hole is directly beyond a dangerous bunker, just left of a pond. Not much room behind the hole, but anything left is a dicey proposition as well.

19

I hit a Gap wedge to six feet.

The ball never left its line, and checked right up. It may have even spun back a touch. Very nicely done. This is a great opportunity to keep this little run going, maybe build a a bulwark of pars or better against the inevitable pullback to come. Even the best golfers in the world sometimes hit the ball poorly. That's why it is essential to take advantage of these chances when they come along.

20

I am not leaving this sort of Birdy Putt short anymore. It's a real simple equation: Good players make more of these. And you can't make more of these if you don't get them to the Hole.

But it misses. Runs a little farther by the hole than I would have liked, too. I may not have taken the downhill slope into proper consideration. That is the danger of getting too bold with these mid-range makeable putts. That was too aggressive.

21

I have 2 and a half feet left for Par. You have got to make these if you want to be any good at all.

I push it just right.

Someone says (correctly), "You stood up on it".

Seething, spitting, frothing animal rage.

*

I once found a perfectly good wooden Red Stripe dartboard case on the street. It was at the corner of 72nd Street and Amsterdam in NYC, and I was on my way home to Queens from The Smith's apartment.

Years later, in a similar mood to that which I find myself on this 5th Green, at 4 o'clock in the morning, I destroyed the dartboard. With a 5-iron.

22

Tap. Deep cleansing breaths, stalk to the next tee.

Greedy greedy greedy. You get greedy and the game pulls you right back in. You go from having an aggressive run at birdie to making bogie. From three strokes to five. In a second of greed.

Ah, fuck it. I am who I am. I have been saying that a lot lately. I had a good look at birdie, so I took a chance and it bit me in the ass. It happens. It never happened. If I keep hitting the fairway, and keep hitting the green, I will have other opportunities.

*

The worst day I ever spent on the golf course was on the course at Dartmouth College. I played poorly on a very tough course, and my (random) playing partners were not to my liking. This last part was unusual. In the dozens of times I have golfed with strangers, I can remember only this one time as being less than pleasant.

*

We have a great time in the Frances Fiolek Memorial Tuesday Night Golf League. It is old school, in the best way. Ball busting is the order of the day, with a side of Beer and Sand Bagging. We have a good bunch of guys, from Salesmen and Contractors to Plumbers and Electricians, with a Mayor, Lawyer, Dentist, Farmer, and Fireman thrown in for good measure. It's not for the faint of heart, or those easily bruised, but it is a damn good time. I hope that my son, Henry, gets to play in the league when he gets to be of age. And since the league has been around for this long, who knows. But I have a sinking feeling that, as most good things do, it might have gone the way of the dodo by then.

*

There is a garage under my office. It has never been used for cars, since the driveway doesn't come within 50 feet of it. The garage has been partially insulated and sheet-rocked, and it has been wired for electric and cable. I have acquired the necessary insulation to finish the job, but I have not had time to install it. Also, I require moral support for this sort of project, and my friend M has not had a free day when I do. When completed, the garage will be the largest room in our 1880 Coachmen's House.

I am looking forward to having the additional living space. For three reasons especially.

1. My office, where I am writing at this very moment (December 12, 2010 12:07 PM), occupies the currently largest room in our house.

2. The garage, while technically part of the structure of the home, can only be accessed from outside. It sits just below my office,

which is connected to the rest of the house via a small staircase off the back of the kitchen.

3. We'll be able to have a dartboard, which will replace the one I destroyed, in a drunken fit at 4 in the morning, in our old apartment in Astoria.

We were going to insulate yesterday, but a few days ago I was offered an opportunity to work/ski at Catamount, up on the Hillsdale, NY, Egremont, MA border. So I got up early, picked up my buddy Frank (who has worked there since he was 18), and spent the next 6 or so hours installing racing gates and fencing, setting up the finish line, then breaking it down again, all while skiing for the first time this season (for me, it was the first time in several seasons). It was good, fun, low-key outdoor work, and an excellent workout. I'm going back again next weekend, and this will hopefully constitute my golf off-season fitness regiment.

Today, Sunday, I'm a bit stiff (but surprisingly not too sore). It's been pouring all day, so the local Ski Areas are closed (including Mohawk, where I'm hoping to teach you, Maggie, to ski next week.).

*

Gotta get a check with a couple commas. One word does not flow to the next like one note flows to the next. Music carries momentum better than prose. Entropy. Once you start playing, I imagine it's easier to keep on playing. Whereas this typing...christ, this a slim little book about a minor event (even my own minor life), but it's like fucking pulling teeth to get one paragraph to lead into the next. Instead it's spinning of the wheels, repeating old stories, typ-procrastinating for hours at a time. At some point, it does make me question whether or not I have anything to say.

If nothing else, I've got to get this thing finished for my kids. With the amount I drink, the relatively high-stress of this particular cash-poor lifestyle, and my genetic predisposition towards paunch...who knows how long I'll be here. I want to leave them something that contains a little bit of whatever little bit of wisdom I may have accidentally come across, as well as a document of One Good Day. Sometimes, that's all we get. I am the brokest paper millionaire in the State of Connecticut. And while I'm grateful for all the blessings I receive, it is starting to get to me. 15 years of this shit...in a normal family that keeps its shit together, I'd be praised and celebrated. In my family, the wife and I get to deal with this shit all by ourselves, with the notable exception of the help her side of the family provides. I mean, christ, kids, it takes a village, right? Well, where the fuck is it. Having created a few million in wealth out of thin air, is it too much to ask that the small percentage of our monthly expenses that aren't covered by cash on hand, be, you know, covered. Childcare is expensive these days, and my clients take way too fucking long to pay their bills.

23

I make a good swing on this 6th tee-box, with the 3-wood/hybrid. This is a Par 5, playing left-to-right, then back to the left again. There is Out-of-Bounds right. Hit hard and higher than usual, and right down the left-center of the fairway. M says, "If I could hit it like that every time, I'd put this away too.", referring to his driver. He hits it a country mile, and is one of the nicest guys you'd ever want to meet. If he continues to improve his short game, he is going to be dangerous.

24

J hit his on the same line, but maybe 50-60 yards farther. So we find ourselves in the woods, contemplating shots I do not have. He's thinking of hitting a 3-wood through a narrow gap in the trees cut 30 or 40 yards over a pond at the green, or a driver off the bark chips through an even tighter hole.   I would most likely be punching a 6-iron back towards the fairway. I grab a 4-iron, and head back to my ball 50 yards behind, but on the same line and in the middle of the fairway.

A little looping drawing liner, but right down the chute. Another case where a shot that is just OK will do just fine. The idea is to make each shot a little easier than the last on any given hole. A Coach friend of mine calls my game "scary good" around the green. So the easiest, simplest way to get in the vicinity seems to be the way we need to approach each hole.

25

I have a gap wedge from 110 yards out. I don't get quite enough of it but the ball winds up on the dance-floor. With a wedge in hand, I really ought to get it 30 feet closer than I did. Though on the previous hole I have just learned that hitting it to 6 feet does not guarantee anything. Maybe a longer putt that I can really lag will get me back into the rhythm I was in prior that unfortunate 3-putt.

26

I have a 25 foot putt. It slides a little right to left.

I make my stroke, and it moves in that direction more than I think, but my putt has good speed. It finishes up about two feet from the hole.

27

I make a good, smooth, abbreviated stroke. Par. Nothing out here that a few more of these wouldn't fix. No bills to pay, no work to do, no drama or tragedy. Just a little fresh air, a little sunshine (sometimes), and a little friendly competition.

Though as you may have noticed, I don't much know what the other guy is doing in any given hole, unless he's where I am. One of the strengths of my game, at this point, is my ability to block out most other external ingame stimuli.

28

This 7th Hole is a Par 3, playing 165 Yards over a pond. I hit a good 6-iron, but the ball stays dangerously above the hole. Maybe 8 feet. Dead down hill, with a little bit of right to left in it.

Get greedy with this one, and it'll go down to the bottom of the hill. But if I don't get it to the Hole, I will still have a downhill putt ahead of me.

29

That last thought must have stayed with us, because I somehow leave the Birdy Putt short.

"How does that stay up there? Really?", I say, in mock-disbelief.

"Thought you gave it enough.", one of the boys says.

No one would think that this putt would have any trouble getting to the hole, but it does. It takes the break and runs out to 2 feet or so right of the hole. Just the sort of little tester that can undermine a pretty good round.

30

Little bit of break on this one, if I die it in the hole. And if I don't die it in the hole, it will probably go 4 feet past. Good putt. Good 3. Grinding it out. Got some impressed looks from the boys.

31

On this 8th Tee I hit a nasty little smother-hook with our 3-wood/hybrid down the left side, and getting lefter by the moment. It's well past the pond though, so I should be able to put a club on it, and get it going towards the green.

I probably should have hit 3-iron off this tee, since anything in the middle of the fairway would give me a short-iron into the green, which lies in a shallow de-elevation. Instead, I am going to have to scramble. This is the sort of situation that calls on the short game to save no worse than bogie from a less-than-ideal (but in play) spot.

32

Easier said than done. I hit a punch with not much of a purpose or solid strike. But I manage to steer it between the correct two trees, so it's at least advanced. 20 yards short of the green, still on the left side. Short-sided ourselves a bit though, as the pin is over here too. Not much room to work with, but better to run it a little long than to dump it, and leave it up here.

33

I have a tight little chip over a hump, from about 20 yards. I didn't have too much room to work with, but I get the ball safely on this 8th green. I really need to grind out no worse than bogie from here. This should have been a birdy hole.

34

I get a little bold with this putt from 15 feet. This leaves us 3 feet out for bogie.

Don't want too many of these in the course of a round. More than a few and you can really start to lose the stroke. Get tentative. Bad for the nerves. Starts to feel ever so slightly more like work. Which, god knows, it ain't.

Not much in this one though. Just need to bring the Heavy Putter back and through, like I have done before. It is a very simple motion, and the Heavy Putter makes it even simpler.

35

I make a good stroke. A good two-putt. Saved a bogie. I don't want too many of these. But make a few of them over the course of a round, and you can turn a mediocre day into something else entirely. Sure as I'm sitting here, I do swear by this Heavy Putter. It is a B2-M. One of the very few clubs for which I have paid full price. It keeps the wrists and hand out of the putting stroke, allowing the golfer to use the larger muscles of the shoulder to get the stick moving back and through. Smoothly.

Though putters don't tend to wear out (unlike wedges and irons), I have two of these putters. Just in case. I'm not sure just in case what. But just in case. It is right here in my office. I also have two extra grips for the putter. I had a leather grip put on the first of the two identical putters I have, but sometime about halfway through this golf season, it was clear that it was necessary to return to the original grip. So, fascinatingly enough, the 2nd of the two identical putters went into play.

36

I pull my 3-wood/hybrid on this 9th Tee, and hit one down the right side. Another low lining draw.

Long way home from here. Playing out of the fairway again though. This is important when I know I am going to have a longer club for my approach shot.

37

I hit a hard 4-iron, into the wind. Gotta at least get it up there in wedge range. I aim it right at that left bunker. Anything short of it will give me a nice angle into the green towards the hole. And I am unlikely to get it to the bunker itself.

Now if I had a reliable wood/hybrid to hit off the deck, that would be something else entirely. It's probably just what I will need to take the next step as a player.

I have made double-bogie on this 9th Hole before, and can do so again in a heartbeat. Stated simply, there is so much pressure to swing hard at the second shot on this hole, especially when one's drive has been less than stellar. I have seen very good players hit very poor shots in just this sort of situation. It's human nature to get tight when one is trying to do something faster or with more force than usual.

38

I hit a Lob Wedge pitch to 12 feet. This is pretty much my bread and butter shot on this sort of hole, so I am usually expecting to scare the hole. This particular pitch is not great, but I shouldn't make worse than 5 from here.

I am keeping it together. Barely. This will be another first putt that will need to have good speed. Get it up there in the neighborhood.

39

I don't put my best stroke on this one, but it had pretty good pace. That putt did not have much chance of going in, but I am left with not much more than a tap-in.

40

Tap.

A frontside 40.

4 over Par.

Not half bad.

The pint of bourbon I usually carry in my bag is sadly absent today. So we head into the clubhouse for a Vodka and Cranberry. I hate to encourage having a touch of the sauce for performance purposes. But a little relaxer sure does clear up some tempo issues in a hurry.

There's something about the time we golfers spend in the clubhouse at the turn, during a semi-serious round, when that's part of the layout of the course. It's like coming back to the bench after a shift on the ice, or back into the dugout after a long inning. We re-gird our loins, change our undershorts when necessary, and get everything we think we may need to finish this thing off.

*

Because you get to a point where you are not looking for a Faster Ride, as the Cartel song goes. Something to be said for Lower Lows and Higher Highs, but not forever. That's why this game has persisted for so many centuries. It replicated some basic, primal, elemental need of semi-civilized men. Hit, find and hit it again. Some sort of hunter gatherer business going on there...the fewest whacks with a stick equates to...what, exactly?

I guess that's what we're all doing out there. The retired old man, the unmarried career girl, the off-duty bartenders, judges, plumbers, electricians, mechanics, firemen, single

mothers, idle rich. The simple act of hitting it, finding it, and

hitting again satisfies some primal urge. Which is why

there were people out there today, on our last day of the

year, November 28th. In 36 degree temperatures. With

smiles on their faces. It beats working, as I always say.

41

I sometimes get vertigo on this 10th tee. This Hole is straight downhill, with a falling away steppe-like tee complex. Just about 75% of this shot is a forced carry over a swamp hazard.

4-iron from 190. Hit well, but comes up a foot or two short of the desired back tier. Probably 3-putt territory. Still, safely on, and the back 9 may be off to a good start.

At this awkward juncture, one of the cart girls, who we all know, pulls up with a smile. I can recall a few choice exchanges that I've had, or witnessed, with these girls, who have become our friends.

"Hello boys".

I say, "If I drop dead, XXXXX, please do speak of me well. Even if you have to lie. Hehehe. I'm ready for ski season. What sort of looks will you be rocking this Wintertime?"

"Whatever. You're a jackass. Stupid clothes. I hate cold weather."

"Now, now, dear. There are few things more delightful in all the world than a well filled-out sweater or fleece. Warms my heart. Right here."

"Will you be changing your hair for the season? I certainly will. Gonna grow out the old afro. It's pretty sweet."

"Nope, I'll stay this color for a while"

"No harm in that. What else is happening?"

"I also have these bites on my chest. And neck."

"Not from me."

"That's hard to say."

"No, it's not. I just said it, and it was easy."

*

"What about that goat you were going to sacrifice? So that I'd get that house I wanted."

"I have become one with the goat. I am him. He is me. I am no longer willing to sacrifice the beast."

"Nevermind...you're a jackass."

"You hate me. "

And who can blame her. I suspect its because I called her a silly, shallow, deranged, confused, tease. But remember, The Breakfast Club tells us that "She's only a tease if what she does gets you hot."

*

"I had a dream that a busty brunette was planning to poison my soup. You wouldn't know anything about that, would you?"

"Is that a funny, or did you really have that dream?"

"What do you think?"

"I got nothing. What would you like?"

"I'll have the soup."

I turned back toward the golf cart, with a little bounce in my step. I had never noticed it until recently, but I apparently bounce when there is golf or whiskey in my future, or other things.

"Let us read what you have thus far," she said.

"No,", I replied.

"My wife asks the same thing. When I am finished, all of you birds can pick and cluck over it all you like. You will all be looking for the same thing."

42

I think its gonna move hard left when it comes up the tier. I've got the right idea. The damn thing almost goes in. An excellent Putt from 3-Putt territory. This is an amazingly efficient way to cut strokes of your score. Make a good first Putt.

43

I have left myself a 4-footer for Par. Fairly straight, a little bit of left to right still in it. Drano. Excellent two-putt. Good start to the back nine. That doesn't always mean anything, but I have had some good scores on this back 9. And the stretch of holes coming up has been especially good to me.

44

Off this 11th tee, I hit my 3-wood/hybrid up the right side again, just short of a hummock. This 360-Yard Par 4 plays straight away, with the road on the far left, and the back end of the Driving Range on the far right. I made not a particularly clean stroke, but safely in play, and probably no more than a 7-iron in to the green.

J and M crush their drives 50 or 80 yards past. J, the much more accomplished player, suggests that M just got him (out-drove him). I express my doubts, though both balls were struck very well, and right in the center of the fairway, no more than a Pitching Wedge into the green. When we eventually get up there it turns out that M had indeed out-driven his younger, more accomplished friend.

45

I have a 7-iron approach up the hill, from about 150.
Sand traps on both sides of the green, and a false front that
repels balls left short, or hit with too much spin. As a result,
one always must take one more club on this particular
approach. I run it up the hill nicely.

46

J misses his Birdy Putt just left. It looked good most
of the way, to me. I ask him whether he tugged it just a
touch. He says yes.

I make a good stroke, with a little knowledge. Too
little, as I miss mine just just right. I may have pushed it
just a touch.

47

Tap-in par. My favorite kind. Good rhythm to that hole. Hit the fairway, hit the green, good putt misses, tap in par. Make the game feel (temporarily) almost easy.

The thing is...the really good players make those Birdy Putts much more often. It doesn't seem like much, but when I think of what making 3 or 4 more of these putts every round would do to my game. Not only would I gain those strokes on the scorecard, but you'd also reap the rewards of having the confidence to really go after certain shots. I do not have this.

Not yet, anyway. This year (2010) was the first of the five years that I have been playing that I sometimes felt that I knew what I was doing. That I could press to make birdy or par, and still stay in enough control to avoid making worse than bogie. Because, as I have said before, bogies are our friend. At this point, and probably for the remainder of our golfing life.

I can make Pars in bunches, and the occasional birdy. Enough to make up for at least some for the bogies we make in the course of a round. It is the double, triple-bogie, more-than-triple bogies that are un-reversable on a scorecard.

48

On this 12th Tee, I hit a 6-iron from 169. I yanked it over to the left side, about hole high and 10 yards or so off the green. I was left with a chip of some 30 feet over a hump, to a relatively flat green.

49

Using my Lob Wedge, I chipped it. Just not close enough. 8-10 feet for Par, with a little bit of left to right break. I definitely need to be more aggressive with these, but I don't want to bring double-bogie into the equation. This is a green that I should usually hit off the tee, so I am definitely losing some ground by having to grind out chips and long putts on this easy downhill Par 3.

50

This putt Misses. Not by much. Sometimes they just don't go into the hole. And that is OK. If you expect more, you are sure to be disappointed, at any level of expertise. The bottom line is that from anything farther than a foot or two, and sometimes even from there, it is a damn difficult thing to get the ball to roll into a little hole. If you are trying.

If you are on one foot, with one hand on the putter, and your eyes closed...it get's easier. Which is why children can sometimes make it look scarily easy.

51

Not a great spot for a bogie, but this tap-in doesn't hurt my cause too much. Tap-in bogies on holes where we make mistakes are not to be taken lightly. Much better for the golfing psyche than those 3 footers we keeping leaving

ourselves.

*

On the wall of the stairwell leading to my office,

there are three team pictures from the 1920s that include

my Grandfather. The only one with a label says Morris

Soccer 1927. There is a P on the jerseys of one of the

other teams, perhaps pertaining to Pelham. There is a

town called Morris right next to us here, but they are not the

same places. These teams were in The Bronx. In the third

picture, the boys are all in shirt and tie, and my

grandfathers tie is tucked into his shirt. I have no idea what

this means.

52

I hit a good 3-wood/hybrid down the right side of this 13th fairway. The ball rolls just off the short stuff, on this narrow, straightaway 350 Yard Par 4. This will leave me with a pretty straightforward approach into this green. But out of this semi-rough, I won't be able to get much spin on the ball. In this situation, I've got to plan on the shot releasing.

53

I hit a punchy little 7-iron from 155 yards. It doesn't quite get to the right tier, but it is a good, straight shot to a fairly narrow green. I am in the neighborhood, so it is imperative that I don't let my concentration lapse.

54

I am putting from 9 feet under the hole, hard left to right up onto the upper tier of this 13th green. I had the right idea, but not enough gas. Must be getting tired. Time for a little bit of that Vodka and Cranberry. If I am going to be tired, and if this is the beginning of the inevitable decline of our play on this day, I might as well do it with a sip of a strong cocktail.

55

Not quite a tap in, but no problem. I make these all day on the good days, without breaking a sweat. Good Par. Make a few more over these next few holes, and I might have something.

56

This 14th Hole is a short 320-yard dogleg right Par 4.
I ain't going over those trees on the right, as I have seen so
many many people try to go over. Some of them succeed.
But very few of them make eagle. And making eagle is the
only reason to attempt the shot over the trees.

In order to setup a good chance at birdie, I have got
to flirt with the right side just a bit. If I hit it hard enough, it
might just catch the slope and setup a make-able chip or
putt for eagle. I do, and it does.

57

Thing is, I am so unfamiliar with something like an
eagle chip that I lose focus. I don't get aggressive, the way
I do with something I need to get up-and-down. Scare the
hole, for christ's sake. Even if you run it too far by, you'll
then know what the putt does coming back.

58

OK. Birdie putt from just off the floor. 12-15 feet, not much in it...maybe a little left to right. Not enough though, as it stays out there.

59

Another tap in par. I like these. Even more than making some of these, the tap ins continue to tell us that I am playing well. Keeping the ball in play, staying out of trouble, finding the fairway and the green with regularity, and making good Putts.

60

Hehehe. What is it about this 15th tee? Yes, it's elevated.

There are good things I can take from the bigger swing I needed to use at Hanah, Newport National, and other places. Being able to combine my usual accuracy with a higher, bigger ball-flight is just the thing I need to improve my long game. That, plus some sort of hybrid or 3-wood or 5-wood off the deck. Just like I had to on all those long Par 4's at Hanah. And the long Par 5's. And the long Par 3's.

The point is that I can make a relatively bigger swing without sacrificing much of the accuracy I require. It's all about keeping the club on line throughout the impact zone, for as long as possible.

There really is something about driving the ball well. I guess that's because it's the part of the game most like baseball or hockey. You get up there and instead of trying to hit it into a circle, you try to hit it as far down a line as possible. Got to square that face though, because when I go after the ball like that, I tend to not let my hands get through the zone. The big right block.

Not this time though. Left side, high, hit hard, and holding its line. I think I finished this year at even Par on this hole.

61

An 8-iron from 133 yards out, to a bowl-shaped green with a cart path circling it. There is a bunker and a swamp on the right, out-of-bounds far left and long. A nice smooth 8 should be just about right. A little long is fine, and avoids the trouble.

62

I am left with 10 feet for birdie. Fairly flat with a little left to right in it. A little more than I thought, and it doesn't quite get to the hole. Something about Birdie putts from this distance though. Just enough in it that I coax it up there, and if it goes in, it goes in. If not I am in the vicinity. I would finish this year at even Par on this 15th Hole

63

One footers for Par. I will take these whenever I can get them. With three holes left, I am in unfamiliar territory. I have not looked at the scorecard. I have a Par 5, a peculiar Par 4, and another Par 5 still to go. Anything could happen if I don't keep my shit together.

64

This might be the most uncomfortable tee box on the course for me. The opposite of the previous Hole. I hit my 3-wood/hybrid at the right side...too far right, and it just barely clears the marsh. A deep breath. I think I have something going here, and a lost ball is still all it would take to fuck things up significantly. Sure is a fine way to spend an afternoon though. Beats working.

65

Off the tee, I was pretty damn sure that my drive had just barely cleared the left edge of the marsh, then rolled a little farther right. But when we get up to my ball, I see that it got some roll out. This is not a bad spot, though I must carry the next shot at least 150 yards to avoid the next swampy area.

This is not a difficult shot, but I get greedy. Again. I push my 5-iron right. I get the shot over all the swampy area, but I hit it so far right that it heads across the cart path, and right behind a tree that is mostly on the 14th Hole.

66

Well. This is a good spot to take a moment. I take a moment to collect myself, and let J. make his way over for a looksee. It's either backwards behind the tree towards the fairway, or up through a possibly imaginary hole in the branches up towards the green.

Fortune favors the bold, and I managed to get it going up in the right direction, undeflected. Good execution of the shot. And lucky. That's the thing about this game, these shots. A foot to the right or left with a shot like that, and you can very easily make 9 or 10. It is not that tough to play this game reasonably well. It is just very easy to play poorly, or to get a bad break. At any point in the hole or round, something can go wrong with tremendous ease.

*

As I sit here writing this, much of the way into this tale, golf season has turned to ski season. The flags, clubs, carts and leaves are long gone, and the greens are covered. The first flurries of the year (real and artificial) have fallen, and I am looking forward to teaching my daughter to ski this year.

It'll be nice to be on the mountain with her on a weekday morning, when there's hardly anyone else out and about. Not to sound like someone I'm not, but it'll give us the opportunity to appreciate the natural beauty of our surroundings, as well as the activity itself. Just like during the golf season.

*

My wife Amey and I went to a Holiday party at the house across the street from our house. Nice people from the city were renting the house for the year. It had 3 or 4 fireplaces, a hideously spectacular view of Mt. Tom and the sunset. A truly lovely place to throw a Holiday party.

We came quite early and left after about 80 minutes. We had a few drinks at the very well appointed bar, chatted somewhat awkwardly with strangers and some other neighbors from both sides of the street. Once the children started to get restless (this includes me), and the friends of the people from the city arrived in numbers, we made our exits and headed home.

67

I have got what looks to me like a Gap Wedge into the green, from the left side of the fairway. I just want to get this one dancing...give me a par putt. This is one of those many occasions when a mediocre shot might still do the trick.

Just give yourself a putt at it. Don't waste a stroke at this late juncture. A halfway good shot here is ten times more useful than trying to do too much, and wasting the stroke altogether.

68

I have 14 feet left for par. The ball will roll somewhat right to left, and almost a little bit downhill. I'm getting nervous, after that near-miss with the tree on my third shot. At this point, I just want to coax this one up there, take a bogie and move on to the 17th Tee. Sometimes, however, when I want to do that, I grip the putter a bit too tightly and leave the ensuing putt woefully short. If I do that here, I'm going to make my first double bogie of the day. And possibly worse.

With this in mind, I make a good putt. It doesn't have much chance of going in, but I don't have much left at all for a 6.

69

Not quite a tap-in, but no problem. A mighty good bogie, considering the parts of the course we saw on this hole. An excellent 6.

70

The tee is a little bit farther back than usual on this 17th Tee, and we merry four are almost a bit into the wind. This is a quirky little dogleft right Par 4 of 307 Yards. I hit the 5-iron, but slip a bit. Poor balance. Also, I should have been hitting the 4. Turned it over right to left too, which is not usually ideal on this hole. I get away with it though. I have hit the ball far enough past the trees on the right to allow us a shot into the narrow green.

71

Another Gap wedge in. Ideally, I'd like to get this ball onto the correct, right-side, higher tier. But anything short and/or left will probably be just fine. And that's exactly where the ball winds up. A little short, and a little left.

72

20 feet for Birdy from just off the collar, up onto the tier with a hard right to left turn. Pace is everything here, and can make the difference between Par and double bogie.

73

Two and half feet. Not much movement in it. Fairly flat too. Don't miss this, or you'll regret it. Good, smooth stroke. Gotta love the Heavy Putter. Par.

74

I have the tee. Without a thought, hearing only the hiss of heavy static, I grab the 3-wood hybrid on this 18th Tee. The tee shot on this uphill 510-yard Par 5 plays fairly straight away, and the landing area for a good shot is just past a short stone wall dropoff, to the main part of the fairway.

On automatic, like I am properly programmed, I tee up the ball, a little higher than usual. I point the mark of the ball, at my intended line, get a good base, take a waggle or two, and pull the trigger. I lace one down the middle, just past the steeplechase drop and waste area. Not too far, but right down the middle.

M says, "Look at that. He doesn't care. He just steps right up and hits it. Straight, too."

I still hear the hiss, but I let go of a breath, and I can feel that I have have no fairways left to hit. Work to be done, though. Let's not fuck it up.

75

In a similar situation, I hit a second shot just like the second shot on 6. A punchy, drawing liner. Right on line, if not exactly crushed. 180 or so yards, finishing in the right-center of the fairway. I'm getting better at these shots. Learning to take plenty of club and take a little off it. Resulting in a nice tight draw that will work in any conditions, on any course.

76

A pitching wedge from 120 yards out. The pin is on the right side, one tier up, over a bunker. Still plenty of opportunity here to do the wrong thing with the golf ball: lose control of it. There's a road to our immediate right.

Some thick vegetation to our right, as well as bunkers short-right, short-left, and long-left.

I thin it a little bit, but got enough of it to get it over all the trouble, and heading in the right direction.

And then it hits me. I don't have any more golf swings to make today. If I can two-putt or three-putt, I'll have done something that I think only 2% of golfers ever do. I will have broken 80.

77

Not so fast. Don't get greedy. All golfers have seen (or heard about) someone getting to this point, close to some goal, or to winning some match or tournament, only to blow it all up on the last green with a careless putt or two. Or three. Or four. Or more.

I have an 8-footer above the hole for birdie. Just trying to coax it up into the general vicinity of the hole, and wrap it all up. Gotta be careful with the speed though...too much of a stroke and the damn thing might run down off the tier, which would put a double bogie or worse into play.

The ball is definitely going to move left to right. Probably a foot or more depending on the speed.

*

As I write this, it's December here in NW CT, and I have skied 2 out of the past 4 days. This roughly doubles my total for the previous 10 years. Unlike golf, I learned early. I was on skis by 4, and we used to ski a dozen or more days a season, for a while. But in the last 20 years, I've been on the hill maybe a dozen times. And boy, this past Saturday...it showed.

Great fun though. Little turns, big turns...I like to keep the variety going. And while I go at a pretty good pace, I don't like to go too fast. I definitely prefer to remain in control, or as close to it as possible under the circumstances.

*

5 days later, and I have skied 6 days out of the past 8. I definitely have not skied this much since I was in middle school, and perhaps not even then. I should almost certainly take tomorrow off. Gotta rest those weary knees and calves. It's addictive though, and I need to go to the mountain anyway, to see if they have a Seasonal Rental Ski that is, ahem, a little longer and a little stiffer. This current pair is all right for a little of this or that, and for the work I do at the mountain (helping to setup and breakdown the race courses), but at speed, and in the corners, they chatter. I'm a bit tentative with speed and steeps anyway, what with all this rust, so the last thing I need is the front half of the ski bouncing all over the goddam place.

*

It is a whole hell of a lot of fun to go along down the mountain, making rhythmatic turns, bouncing and stepping bounce and forth, smoothly. Gliding along on that edge sharpens the senses, and frees the mind. You need to pay attention, and you need to think of nothing.

The Banquet

As I mentioned in the beginning, tonight is the Banquet for the Francis Fiolek Memorial Tuesday Night Golf League. This was my first year in the league, but it has been going on since the 1960s. I had a great meal, busted balls with a good bunch of guys for several hours, and I won $57, for finishing in a tie for 2nd in Points among the A Players. Woohoo.

Later that evening, J and I to retired The Block, a bar in town. Your babysitter, P, drank too much and backed her sports car into her garage, while attempting to park.

The End

There is a tree behind our house. In the 4 1/2 years we have been here, it is always the last one in the neighborhood to turn yellow, then red, then brown, and shed its leaves. Every other tree visible from this big window that looses its leaves, has done so. This one (a Maple?), has finally started to go these last few days.

It's November 10, and the leaves on the topmost part of the tree have turned colors, and begun to fall off. The leaves in the middle of the tree have mostly turned their colors, but mostly remain. Those on the bottom have just begun to turn.

*

I had a great season. Met my performance goals, made some great new friends, and had fun. I missed our last tournament of the season, though, and I regret it terribly. The night before, a Saturday, I had walked down to the bar, as I do from time to time. A friend who was to be my playing partner in the morning, and his buddies, had come by shortly after I arrived, and we had a good time. I had three drinks. Not too much for me.

When I got home, I spent much of the evening quite ill, and eventually threw up, and passed into a deep sleep.

I missed my tee-time, as did my playing partner. We were both still ill well into the next afternoon. But still, sorry boys, that was a bush league move. I speak for both of us when I say that it was not our finest moment.

78

Take a deep breath. Don't fuck this up. And stop thinking about it...just focus. FOCUS.

Two practice strokes, head down, trust it...comes off at good pace, moves right, a little more, par.

Plenty of people play golf their whole lives without playing as well as I did today.

And I didn't do anything today that I don't normally do. I just did it at a better pace, a higher level, than ever before. I think I can do this again. Maybe not all the time, but at the very least on a somewhat regular basis.

*

This was the first time I had shot in the 70s at a Par 72 18-Hole layout. I had actually broken 80 a few times previous to this round, including a 77. But those were 18-Hole Rounds at my 9-hole, Par 70 Course. This very first time was actually a consecutive 39 and a 40, separated by an evening. So while that counts for one's Handicap...it didn't really count for me.

A few days after the round in this book, I shot 75 at my home course. That currently stands as my lowest score relative to Par.

Common Greens

I have played, and putted, with mayors, judges, public servants, private investors, minors, the elderly, the unemployed, the unemployable, the attractive, the eccentric, family, friends, friends of family, and everything in between. It is the same for us all. We have to use some sort of stick to roll a ball into a hole.

Nothing we've done before, nothing we'll do eventually, the opinions of those who love us or hate us, or worse yet, ignore us or are unaware of us altogether, matters whatsoever. Not to sound like someone I'm not, but it is those common greens that make this game such a transcendent experience. At its best, it brings people together as people. Not as jobs or family roles or tax brackets or anything else. On those greens, we are all we have in common.

*

Before I ever stepped foot on a golf course, when I lived in Queens, had just been married, and only recently had acquired a rudimentary set of golf clubs, I used to take the five mile trip from my apartment at 34th Street and Broadway in Astoria, to the Randalls Island Driving Range.

I would start by going NW on Broadway, then take a right at 31st Street, where the subway went overhead. In 7/10s of a mile, I'd make an illegal left run onto I-278, which at that point merges onto the Triborough Bridge. In about 2 miles I would then take the right exit toward Randalls Island, among other locales. I would stay straight to go onto the Robert F Kennedy Bridge, and pay a toll. I would then merge onto the ROBERT F KENNEDY via the ramp on the left toward I-278/BRONX/QUEENS/RANDALLS ISLAND.

I would hit balls until fully soaked in sweat. All Fall I'd head over to the range, get myself a Jumbo Bucket, and try to stroke the ball, straight, with some authority. I had hit a few buckets in the few years prior to that Fall, but had never stepped foot on a golf course, and had no history with the game.

Prior to that time, my main source of recreation was thrice-weekly visits to the local batting cage. I would rent the machine for half an hour, have the attendant put the machine on 80 miles per hour, and swing away. I could hit the ball well, from both sides of the plate. When focused, I would swing through no more than half a dozen or so balls in a half-hour session.

Unfortunately, this was poor preparation for hitting a golf ball. When I started out, I had, not surprisingly, a wicked slice. I would hit the ball hard, but late, and the energy imparted to the ball would take it outwards...then swiftly to the right. A common issue for beginner golfers.

After a week or two of trial and error, I found that opening my stance, so effective for hitting a baseball to the left side, was a surefire way to ensure that one's goflball started out left. And swiftly headed right. And farther right.

Still farther. Making a big swoop from its original line,

finishing 70, 70, 90, 100 yards right of the intended target.

Good stuff...unless you are trying to hit the ball straight.

Eventually, it became clear that the power stance

for hitting a golfball was with the left foot slightly closer than

the right (for a right handed player). Pending the

necessary release of the hands (wrists), a squared-up

stance with the front foot slightly ahead of the rear was the

ticket to straights-ville. Clearly, it wasn't going to matter

how hard I hit the ball, if the ballflight took that banana

shape every time we tried to give it a little gas.

*

Ultimately, to play the game at a high level, the

player must be able to turn the ball one way or another as

the situation demands. Not unlike that of a skilled

wordsmith. No harm can come from having a preferred

ballflight. It's good to have a goto pitch when one

absolutely needs the ball in play. But that's the thing about this silly game: wicked slice, brutal hook under pressure, untimely top. It can all be made to work if one has the right attitude and comportment.

*

It is nearly midnight. It is time for me to take my Xanax, and in a little while head to bed. Probably in about an hour and a half. If I stay up past that point (1:30), the work tends to deteriorate, and so does my mood the next day. Today is Tuesday, November 23rd. At least for another 5 and a half minutes or so. Right at the moment...ah, nevermind what music is playing and what I have had to drink. Do your own thing, with your own beverages, tunes, and medium. When I'm gone, that is what I'd want. Within reason.

www.ingramcontent.com/pod-product-compliance
Lightning Source LLC
Chambersburg PA
CBHW032137040426
42449CB00005B/286